HERE TODAY · PORTRAITS OF OUR VANISHING SPECIES

HERE TODAY

PORTRAITS *of* OUR VANISHING SPECIES

SUSAN MIDDLETON & DAVID LIITTSCHWAGER

Chronicle Books · San Francisco

Printed in Japan.

Library of Congress Cataloging-in-Publication Data

Middleton, Susan, 1948-
Here today: portraits of our vanishing species / Susan Middleton, David Liittschwager.
p.   cm.
ISBN 0-8118-0041-5 (hb). — ISBN 0-8118-0028-8 (pb)
1. Endangered species — United States — Pictorial works.
2. Endangered plants — United States — Pictorial works.
I. Liittschwager, David. II. Title.
QH76.M525S 1991
574.5'29'0973022 — dc20   91-13547
                              CIP

Book interior, design by Reverb / W.L.
Typeset in Berthold Akzidenz Grotesk and Janson Antiqua
by EllaType, Los Angeles, California

Distributed in Canada
by Raincoast Books
112 East Third Avenue
Vancouver, B.C. V5T 1C8

10 9 8 7 6 5 4 3 2 1

Chronicle Books
275 Fifth Street
San Francisco, California 94103

To the memory of
Charles Robert Middleton and Frank Richardson,

whose love for the Earth and all its creatures remains a powerful example.

Table of Contents

6

BLACK AND WHITE PORTRAITS | COLOR PORTRAITS

on the cover ··17 | —
scale .60x

Species Descriptions
by Gordy Slack

by Wendell Berry

8

It is now generally understood that the fate of creatures is inextricably linked with the fate of places. When we destroy a habitat, we destroy the creatures who inhabit it. When we destroy a kind of habitat, we destroy a kind of creature—a species.

All the creatures pictured in this book are members of endangered species. And yet the photographers have rigorously excluded any trace or hint of habitat. It is useful to ask why.

This intense concentration upon the appearance of the creature itself is, to begin with, a plea. It is a way of saying, Look! Look! See how fearfully and wonderfully this creature is made. See how beautifully the feathers, or the scales, or the short smooth hairs are laid together. See the gloss of live intelligence in this eye, and in this one. See how elegantly shaped and veined is this flower. See with what power this tree has lifted up its little leaves.

It is a way also of saying: By this intricacy, this supreme delicacy and elegance, understand that neither you nor a multitude of you could make such a creature. If you could make even a replica, you could not make it live. If it did not exist, you could not imagine it. Since it does exist, please do not neglect to imagine it.

By asking us to see only the creature, or one aspect of the creature, the photographers also are confessing to a limit of photography, and to a limit of sight and understanding. A creature's habitat cannot be adequately seen in the one look of a photograph, or in many looks of the unmediated eye. The creature is to some degree shaped by its habitat; its habitat is to some degree shaped by it. The habitat of any creature is also the habitat of other creatures. A creature lives in relation not just to the static place that we tend to suggest by the word "habitat," but to an ever-changing pattern of influences and responses that none of us will ever adequately see or understand.

No more can we see, without destroying it, the system beneath the skin that shapes the creature from the inside, as its ecosystem shapes it from the outside. We *cannot* see it all. To us, its being will never be entirely separable from its mystery.

But something of what can be seen can be shown, and here is the reason for this book. What we can see can be offered to us in such loving particularity as to cause us to intuit or anticipate the intricacy of the whole. If this is the form of the creature, how manifold and wonderful must be the forms by which it lives! The visible, rightly shown and rightly seen, can compel our reverence for what we cannot see.   *April 17, 1991*

Our ability to perceive quality in nature begins, as in art, with the pretty.

It expands through successive stages of the beautiful

to values as yet uncaptured by language....   ALDO LEOPOLD

by Susan Middleton

In 1983 a pair of endangered fringe-toed sand lizards *(Uma inornata)* were brought to my studio to be photographed. I attempted to visually recreate their natural habitat and filled a large tray with sand. A studio light made a semblance of sunlight. They blended into this environment all too well, nearly matching its color and partly burying themselves in the sand. It was effective camouflage, but I wanted to see more. After exposing several rolls of film I lifted them out of the sand, removed the tray, and placed them on a piece of black velvet. Each one of their fringed toes became visible. The leopardlike pattern on their skin, muted in the sand, became vibrant. The outline of their forms was stunning against the black.

The second method, I realized, worked conceptually as well as esthetically. By visually isolating them, I was removing the lizards from exactly what their survival depends upon, which is habitat. What is missing from the photographs against the black is what needs to be preserved to save these lizards from extinction: their environment is emphasized by its exclusion. The lizards are rendered naked, revealing their beauty and uniqueness.

When the photographs of *Uma* taken in the sand were published, they drew the attention of Kelly Cash of The California Nature Conservancy. She wanted to use them in the Conservancy's campaign to secure land in Coachella Valley, California, the lizard's last remaining habitat. On a hunch, I showed her the photographs taken against the black and she responded enthusiastically, recognizing these as the strongest images. The Conservancy used the portraits in their campaign to acquire what is now a fourteen-hundred-acre natural preserve outside of Palm Springs, California.

In 1986 the Conservancy invited me to photograph two more endangered species — the San Joaquin kit fox and the San Joaquin antelope squirrel. At this point I asked David Liittschwager, a former colleague then living in New York, to be technical advisor. He agreed, and we packed a rental van with photographic equipment and set off for the Bakersfield Living Museum, where some of these endangered animals lived. We photographed for three days with the assistance of Gary Parker, one of the museum's animal keepers. He was our go-between with the animals; his predictions of how they would react to us proved entirely true.

David built a Plexiglass studio box with a hatch door for the squirrel, who was lightning fast and a real trick to handle. The squirrel managed to escape by leaping through the hatch door. Four of us chased him for a half-hour before cornering and finally capturing him. Once secured he was a wonderful subject, displaying lots of personality and a wide range of gestures.

We worked with the fox for an entire day in a jerry-rigged enclosure made of plywood. At first he paced back and forth sniffing every spot. I was struck by the exquisite beauty of this animal as we observed him hour after hour. I wanted to touch him, to feel his fur, but he did not want to be touched. He was still essentially wild, even though captive. What he did allow, after nine or ten hours, was for us to settle in close, until our camera and lights were only a foot away from his nose.

As I increasingly appreciated the importance of these

photo: Kelly Cash

endangered creatures, I considered our motivations for photographing them. Was subjecting them to our photographic process fair? We took pains in every case to safeguard the animals and plants and were always accompanied by biologists. Still, would the long-term value of these images we made outweigh the short-term manipulation of each individual? If the work could bring some of these lesser known threatened species to people's attention then it seemed worthwhile. Was it possible that these photographs would come back to haunt us as records of what once was? These and other questions of our species' relationship to wildlife remain with us to this day.

Kelly and I were excited by the pictures of the fox and the squirrel and immediately drafted a proposal to do more photographs of California's endangered species. This led to a comprehensive project sponsored by the California Nature Conservancy in collaboration with the California Academy of Sciences. The Conservancy provided funding to cover expenses, the Academy underwrote the production of an exhibit, and David and I donated our time.

The Conservancy guided the species selection, choosing thirty candidates out of a pool of twelve hundred imperiled species. They were to represent plants as well as animals with particular attention given to species from the most diminished habitats. Other criteria considered in the selection process were urgency, prominence, and accessi-

Santa Ana River Woollystar   May 24, 1988

bility. Some of the species selected have little chance of survival, while others, such as the brown pelican, show how sensitive action can bring a species back from the brink of extinction. Our premise was that every living thing possesses its own unique character and no species would be rejected for lack of charisma. Better known, more glamorous species, such as the San Joaquin kit fox and peregrine falcon, were included. The intent was to represent the diversity of species still existing in the wild.

We photographed in living museums, zoos, motel rooms, in the van, in the wild, under freeways, surrounded by housing developments, near shopping centers, in a farmer's field, next to military runways, by shooting ranges, in a sand and gravel pit, under a transmission tower, and in a horse pasture.

Sometimes we borrowed and photographed animals being researched by biologists. Two barefoot geckos were brought to our motel room in San Diego. We photographed three black toads in my apartment. Only rarely were we in beautiful wilderness areas. More often we photographed in places pressed by development and encroaching insensitivity. We photographed the Santa Ana River woollystar in a sand and gravel pit east of Los Angeles with a freeway behind us, an airport runway next to us, with sand and gravel trucks whipping by and throwing up dust on a 110 degree morning. This area was also used as a refuse dump and was scattered with old couches, mattresses, refrigerators, and tires. The woollystar does not count for much in this environment where stronger forces are taking over its home.

All of these species presented logistical challenges. Some of the species are quite remote, and photographing them required the hard work and cooperation of many people. A biologist studying the Shasta crayfish put on diving gear and searched for the crayfish, carefully distinguishing it from its more aggressive look-alike, which inhabits the same waters near Lake Shasta. We needed cold, clear water for the crayfish to swim in, so while we photographed it she made repeated trips to the center of the pond, hauling buckets of water back to our van.

To photograph the Little Kern golden trout we traveled to Sequoia National Forest, where the Department of Fish and Game had agreed to supply the fish. We prepared a fish studio on the front porch of a local lodge, setting up a custom-built aquarium, strobe lighting, generator, aerated plastic buckets, black and white backgrounds, and a large supply of bottled spring water. We tested the setup with hybrid fish: golden trout mixed with rainbows, the common variety in the area. Meanwhile a team from the Department of Fish and Game was traveling by llama train to an elevation of ten thousand feet to net the pure goldens. In two days they returned with a bucket containing a half-dozen dazzling gold fish with brilliant red stripes along their sides and blue-black spots on their backs — a sight to behold! After a photo session that lasted well into the night we packed the van, including the trout, and drove to a hatchery, where the fish became part of a breeding program to restock mountain streams.

One of the most enjoyable sessions was with the brown pelican at San Diego Sea World. The once wild bird had been injured and had recovered in the park's rehabilitation program. We set up a backdrop and photographed the pelican for five hours. It assumed an amazing variety of positions, from outstretched wings to a crouching, boatlike

photo: Susan Middleton

Shasta Crayfish   August 13, 1990

photos: Kelly Cash

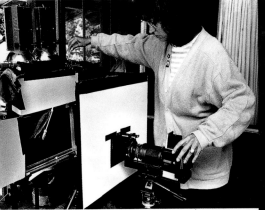

Little Kern Golden Trout   June 22, 1988

posture. It opened and closed its beak creating a sound like clacking bamboo. When we finished photographing it we had the pleasure of witnessing its release.

California Brown Pelican   July 30, 1987

In the two years between September of 1986 and September of 1988 we traveled more than seven thousand miles to photograph these rare species. A traveling exhibition, consisting of twenty-five thirty-eight-inch-square color dye transfer prints, opened at the Academy in December, 1988. During the summer and fall of 1990, with the assistance of Pacific Gas and Electric Company, David and I photographed seven more threatened species on PG&E land. Every subject was photographed in color and black and white, resulting in two very different groups of photographs, both represented in this book.

Most of the animals and plants illustrated here are unknowns, unlike the panda of China or the rhino of Africa, which are universally known and promoted. Perhaps pho-

tography can be a conduit through which these little-known species reveal themselves to people who would otherwise never see them. We want to popularize these animals and plants, and to express their plight because they cannot speak for themselves.

The photograph must be faithful to the integrity of what is before the lens. We begin with a respect for our subjects. Of course we do not know how they perceive us in these situations. When I do portraits of people they are aware of it and can be directed; there is communication. An animal or plant is not self-conscious in the same way, and certainly does not respond to direction. All that we can do is sit still, be prepared, watch carefully, and wait. Sometimes for hours, sometimes days. Yet in a mysterious way it is a collaborative process. The animals reveal themselves through their behavior, which is a kind of performance. In many instances, such as with the great gray owl and the kit fox, there was definitely an interaction, a recognition. Plants present a special challenge because they are passive, their behavior is covert.

We are concerned with rendering exceptional detail by combining aspects of scientific documentation and portraiture. The photographs are intended to convey an intimacy, often through eye contact, with these threatened creatures. They are also meant to be provocative, to sound the alarm.

These photographs are of endangered species living in California, the most species-rich region in America. It has provided fertile ground for a diverse array of life forms many of which occur nowhere else. We humans also have found California alluring, for its climate, abundant natural resources, beauty, and economic opportunities. Because we are the dominant species we proliferate while other living organisms diminish. As the human population increases, pressures on wildlife intensify. The creatures we are crowding out of existence share our home, and for this reason we have a special responsibility to them.

The key to preserving species is preserving ecosystems upon which they depend. The solution is not so much a matter of the preservation of individual species as it is of protecting biological diversity, including natural communities, ecosystems, and regional landscapes. By preserving habitats we can prevent species from becoming endangered. The photographs are meant to draw attention to the underlying problem: the destruction of habitat, of suitable refuge.

We are undergoing an epidemic of extinction and it is caused largely by human development in conflict with wilderness. In the last two hundred years more of California's animals and plants have become endangered than in the last ten thousand years. Not since the extinction of the dinosaurs, sixty-five million years ago, has such a mass extinction occurred. What is hard to comprehend is just how the future of our species is linked to the preservation of biological diversity, the variety of life and its processes.

Desert Bighorn Sheep   June 24, 1988

photo: Kelly Cash

One thing is sure: for us to be healthy, the land must be healthy. We are not separate from nature, we are an integral part of it. But we have become so disconnected from other living beings, so involved in controlling and dominating our environment to provide our so-called high standard of living, that we have lost sight of ourselves as responsible members of the larger community of life on Earth. This alienation threatens the human spirit. Are we the ultimate predators, who with increasingly more powerful means will be able to devour the Earth only to find ourselves endangered? Or do we have the strength, insight, and resolve to adapt our behavior in the best interest of the Earth and of ourselves?

What has become clear is that our relationship to wildlife is neither simple nor static. Historically it has evolved from a life integrated with the natural world, where myths and spiritual sustenance were rooted in nature. It has become a relationship largely based on dominance and exploitation. I hope these photographs will encourage a reexamination of our place within the community of life on Earth and suggest one founded on compassion.

16

Light-Footed Clapper Rail

Feeding mostly on snails, insects, crustaceans, tadpoles, and small fish, the light-footed clapper rail constructs its cordgrass nests under clumps of pickleweed in Southern California's marshlands. Once common from Santa Barbara to the Bay of San Quentin in Baja California, the bird is now limited mainly to six U.S. marshes. About 75 percent of its habitat has been diked and developed. Water pollution and heavy predation by introduced species also plague the bird. There may have been as many as 700 pairs of the rails in the 1970s, but by the last census, in 1986, only 143 pairs remained. Several marshes in the bird's historic range have been restored or are under restoration. The bird's recovery is being aided by floatable nesting platforms that protect nests during breeding season.

Rallus longirostris levipes

ENDANGERED: California
United States

PHOTOGRAPHED: San Diego
July 30, 1987

< San Joaquin Kit Fox

Vulpes macrotis mutica

THREATENED: California
ENDANGERED: United States

PHOTOGRAPHED:
Bakersfield
November 1, 1986

The San Joaquin kit fox emerges from its den at sunset and hunts through the night. The smallest North American member of the dog family, it was once common on the dry plains of the San Joaquin Valley. By 1971 all but seven percent of its original habitat had been lost to residential and agricultural development. Because each kit fox requires about one square mile of territory, protecting the species is difficult. A 1975 survey estimated that fewer than seven thousand individuals remained. Lands have been set aside to protect the kit fox, but it is unclear whether these will be sufficient to sustain the species into the next century.

True to their name (*aquabonita* means beautiful water) the shimmering Little Kern golden trout are perhaps the most beautiful of all trouts. Prized by sport fishermen, these fish are largely restricted to the high altitudes of the Little Kern River Basin in Sequoia National Forest and Park in Tulare County. Nonnative rainbow trout have been introduced to much of the area, resulting in hybridization. Luckily, impassible fish barriers are common throughout the Little Kern River Basin, so some pure stocks of Little Kern golden trout were isolated and preserved. The U.S. Department of Fish and Wildlife is now removing introduced fish from the drainage to make room for the reintroduction of golden trout. By 1990 about 60 percent of the drainage had been restocked with pure golden trout.

Little Kern Golden Trout

Oncorhynchus aquabonita whitei

THREATENED: California
United States

PHOTOGRAPHED: Sequoia National Forest
June 22, 1988

This showy, perennial herb is found on sites near the southern perimeter of Humboldt Bay, in Humboldt County. Cursed by its beauty, the western lily's bulbs have been overcollected. Cattle grazing has also stressed the plant, but habitat loss is its worst problem. There are now fewer than ten known sites where the western lily grows, though recent monitoring and protection efforts have helped stem its decline.

Western Lily

ENDANGERED: California

PHOTOGRAPHED: Humboldt County
June 13, 1987

Lilium occidentale

North American River Otter

Lutra canadensis

Trappers coveted the river otter's thick, soft fur; the animal was one of the great incentives for the exploration of California prior to the gold rush. Fun-loving river otters often play on mudslides they construct on streambanks. They can move sixty-pound loads using their heads and bodies as wedges, and they use their whiskers to feel out crayfish, frogs, fishes, and other favorite foods. The river otter is now threatened by relentless riverside development, water diversion, and dams.

PROTECTED: California
United States

PHOTOGRAPHED:
San Diego
December 10, 1987

Barefoot Banded Gecko

Coleonyx switaki

Also known as the magic gecko, this lizard was not discovered until 1974. It originally lived in the lush rainforests of prehistoric Southern California but was forced to adapt as rainforest turned to desert. Now it occupies only very small, specialized microhabitats in the boulder-strewn desert foothills, where it spends most of its life deep in rock crevices and subterranean chambers. Only five of these habitats are known in the Southern Californian desert. This species, always rare, is vulnerable to illegal collecting. Luckily Anza-Borrego Desert State Park includes some barefoot gecko habitat where the lizard is protected.

THREATENED:
California
United States

PHOTOGRAPHED:
San Diego
December 11, 1988

San Joaquin
Antelope Squirrel

Ammospermophilus nelsoni

This Central Valley squirrel forages and hunts during the hottest times of day, while most mammals rest. When it reaches its temperature limit it darts into a burrow and flattens itself, spread-eagled against the cool earth, unloading its heat. It once lived on 3.4 million acres of arid grass-land, but agricultural development usurped eighty percent of that area, and what re-mains is mostly in bits too small to main-tain self-sustaining populations for long. Ranchers and farmers also poison ground squirrels, considering them pests. The Nature Conservancy and other public organizations have bought lands on the Carrizo Plain for a natural preserve that will protect the antelope squirrel.

THREATENED:
California
CANDIDATE:
United States

PHOTOGRAPHED:
Bakersfield
November 2, 1986

28

Geysers' Panicum

Dichanthelium lanuginosum var. thermale

Unique to the geysers in Sonoma County,
this extraordinary grass has adapted to
high acidity and soil temperatures and
thrives in the hydrothermally altered soil
surrounding the geysers. Geysers' panicum
was always rare, growing in only seven
known locations. Geothermal energy proj-
ects have significantly reduced its populations. Public agencies are working with the
utility companies to protect the geysers'
panicum population in the Little Geysers
Natural Area, which harbors a large
population of the plant.

ENDANGERED: California
CANDIDATE: United States

PHOTOGRAPHED: the Geysers in Sonoma County
July 2, 1990

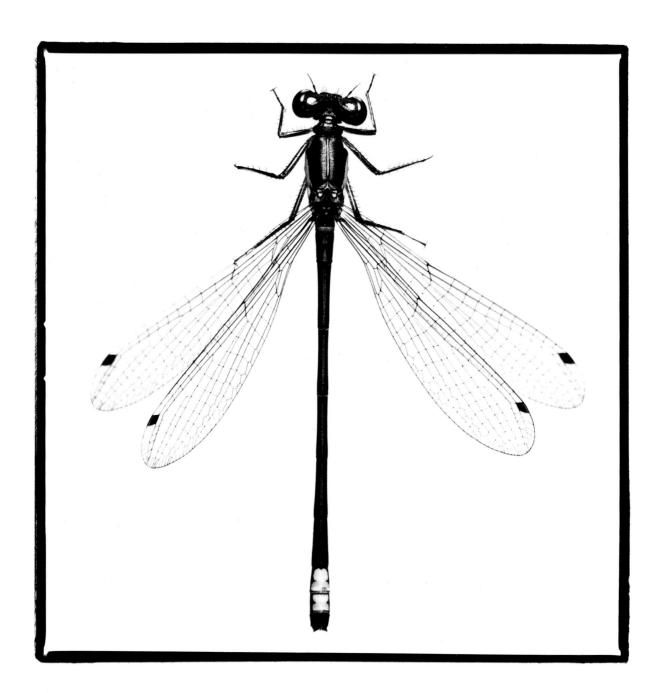

San Francisco Forktail Damselfly

Ischnura gemina

LEFT: Dorsal
RIGHT: Ventral

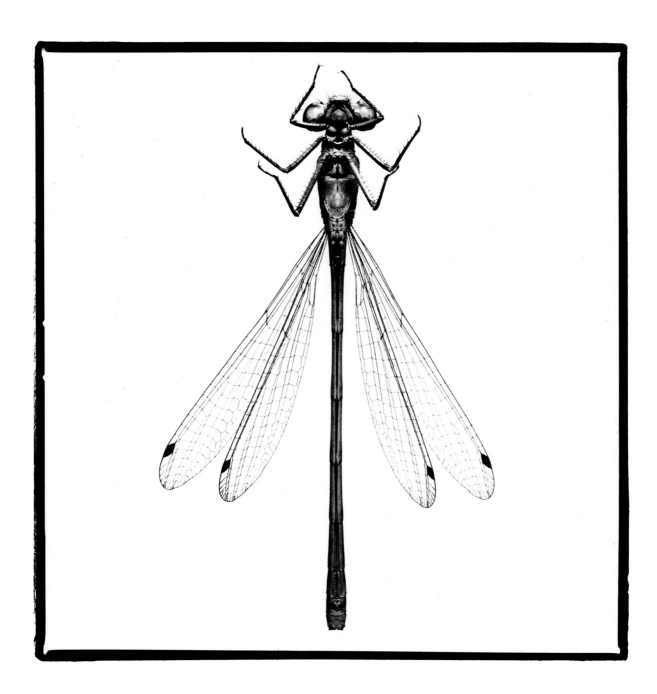

Immature damselflies, called naiads, live in the water and feed on the larvae of mosquitos and other insects and small invertebrates. At about six weeks old they transform into adults and begin to fly, but they remain close to the ponds and slow-moving streams of their origin. Males of this species are bright blue, females a brassy, brownish green. All but one of the damselfly's known habitats are threatened by urban development. There are currently no efforts to protect this species.

CANDIDATE: California
United States

PHOTOGRAPHED: San Francisco
May 28, 1988

Valley Oak

Quercus lobata   One of the largest oaks in the world, sometimes a hundred feet tall, the valley oak
was once commonly found from Los Angeles
to Mendocino. The presence of these huge
trees tipped off early Californians to the
presence of deep, rich, farmable soils, and
settlers began felling them by the thousands
before the turn of the century. Hundreds
of square miles of valley oak forests were
cleared and transformed into agricultural
and residential land. Even today three-
hundred-year-old valley oaks are cut when
they appear to impede progress. No re-
strictions currently protect the trees.

NATURAL COMMUNITY OF SPECIAL CONCERN:
California

PHOTOGRAPHED:
the Central Valley
June 17, 1988

Falco peregrinus anatum

American Peregrine Falcon

Possibly the fastest animal in the wild, the fierce American peregrine falcon may achieve speeds of two hundred miles per hour while diving for prey. Once ranging throughout North America, the peregrine was hard hit by DDT contamination, and by 1970 only two known pairs remained in the state. The pesticide was banned in 1972 and breeding programs have nursed the population up to the eighty pairs now nesting in California. But DDT still taints the food chain, inhibiting the bird's ability to reproduce.

ENDANGERED:
California
United States

PHOTOGRAPHED:
San Francisco
June 10, 1987

39

THREATENED:
California
CANDIDATE:
United States

PHOTOGRAPHED:
San Francisco
May 28, 1988

Endemic to only a few small pools in Inyo County's Deep Springs Valley, this small black toad emits a faint, high squeak rather than the deep vibrating sound of most toads. It slides down rodent burrows or finds hollows under pond banks for its winter hibernation. The desert frog has always been rare, but diversions of water from natural springs, the introduction of carp, and the trampling of streams and ponds by grazing cattle threaten its existence. Attempting to protect its habitat, the California Department of Fish and Game has bought 719 acres of black toad territory in Deep Springs Valley.

Black Toad   Bufo exsul

Salt Marsh Harvest Mouse

Reithrodontomys raviventris

ENDANGERED:
California
United States

PHOTOGRAPHED:
Palo Alto
October 23, 1990

The salt marsh harvest mouse has become the mascot of California's vanishing wetlands. Endemic to the salt marshes of Suisun, San Pablo, and south and central San Francisco bays, this highly specialized mouse is distinguished by its ability to float for long periods during high tides, eat pickleweed, and drink salty marsh water. Its habitat has yielded to airports, dumps, salt farms, and industrial and housing developments. The mouse is also especially vulnerable to nonnative predators. Its population now numbers in the low thousands. Efforts to preserve the mouse on the San Francisco Bay National Wildlife Refuge have been moderately successful, and the refuge's attempts to acquire and restore lost marshland present hope for its survival.

Almost identical to its ancestors of forty
million years ago, the outlandish California
brown pelican winters and breeds on
offshore islands in Southern California and
in Baja California. Each summer and fall
it follows migrating fish north as far as
Vancouver Island. DDT almost annihilated
the species in the United States, causing
the birds to lay brittle, thin-shelled eggs
seldom surviving incubation. The 1972
U.S. ban on DDT gave the brown pelican a
second chance. Oil spills, overfishing, and
human intrusion on breeding populations
continue to plague the bird, but its numbers
have risen dramatically and the federal
government may downlist the brown pelican
from endangered to threatened status.

California Brown Pelican

Pelecanus occidentalis californicus

ENDANGERED:
California
United States

PHOTOGRAPHED:
San Diego
July 30, 1987

California Brown Pelican, Pelecanus occidentalis californicus

45

The woollystar is able to live in the harsh, dry, salty soil of the Santa Ana River's flood plain terraces. The fine, woolly hair covering on its leaves helps it conserve water. The woollystar, one of the ten most endangered plants in the state, has been in dramatic decline over the last decade and its habitat continues to disappear. The channeling of the Santa Ana River, and urban construction up to its edges, have eliminated the plant from most of its original range. Surviving populations are threatened by active and proposed sand and gravel mining on Bureau of Land Management land.

Santa Ana River Woollystar

Eriastrum densifolium ssp. sanctorum

ENDANGERED: California
United States

PHOTOGRAPHED:
San Bernardino
May 24, 1988

Shasta Crayfish

Pacifastacus fortis

The Shasta crayfish evolved and thrived for more than a million years in crystal-clear pools and channels filled with cool spring water until two aggressive, nonnative crayfish were introduced to its habitat. Since 1978 more than half of the Shasta crayfish's range, a small portion of the Pit River Basin in northeastern California, has been lost to its exotic competitors. Habitat degradation also plagues the crayfish; harmful sedimentation results from cattle grazing, logging, forest fires, and nonnative muskrats who burrow in the riverbank. The Shasta crayfish survives best in the colder headwater areas, to which it is better adapted than the introduced species. The Fish and Wildlife Service recommends controlling the nonnative species as well as the causes of sedimentation.

ENDANGERED:
California
United States

PHOTOGRAPHED:
Spring Creek, Shasta County
August 13, 1990

This bottom-dwelling fish sits completely motionless, sometimes hiding under rocks or vegetation, waiting to pounce on unsuspecting prey. The rough sculpin is limited to spring-fed pools and channels in a small portion of the Pit River Basin in northeastern California. Grazing, erosion from logging, and the introduction of nonnative muskrats that burrow in the riverbanks have mucked up the clear river environments the rough sculpin needs to survive. Attempts to minimize riverbank destabilization in its habitat have begun, and the fish's numbers appear to be stable.

THREATENED: California
CANDIDATE: United States

PHOTOGRAPHED: Crystal Lake, Shasta County
September 17, 1990

Rough Sculpin

Cottus asperrimus

This anomalous cactus occurs only in an area near Bakersfield receiving cold winter rains. Most cacti need warm desert ground to put forth shoots. A closely related species contains compounds that appear to be helpful in treating cancer. *Treleasei* has not yet been tested for this quality. Once blanketing the sandy plains around Bakersfield each spring with their stunning fuchsia flowers, these cacti now grow only in patches that shrink yearly, having been displaced by agriculture, residential development, and sand and gravel mining.

Bakersfield Cactus

Opuntia basilaris var. treleasei

ENDANGERED:
California
United States

PHOTOGRAPHED:
Bakersfield
April 20, 1987

ENDANGERED: California
United States

PHOTOGRAPHED: Antioch
May 15, 1990

Antioch Dunes Evening-Primrose   Oenothera deltoides var. howellii

Few witness the one-night flowering of the Antioch Dunes evening-primrose. In the early evening its flowers unfurl. With the coming of daylight they briefly blush and then wilt. Most of the sandy soils of eastern Contra Costa County, which made up its original habitat, have been disturbed by sand mining, off-road vehicles, and industrial and residential development. The plant's only persisting natural stands are found in two small sites within the Antioch Dunes. In 1980 the U.S. Fish and Wildlife Service acquired most of the site and began managing the rest, which is currently owned by the Pacific Gas and Electric Company. By 1988 the population had risen from a little more than 1,000 plants to 4,320.

Sage of the California desert, this ancient tortoise has changed little in the last twenty million years. Though the desert tortoise still occupies most of its original greater Mojave and Sonoran Basin desert range, a barrage of threats has greatly reduced its numbers. Off-road vehicles, hunters, ravens, energy and mineral development, and livestock have all ganged up on the desert tortoise. Recently *Gopherus agassizii* has also been hard hit by a respiratory infection probably introduced through released pets. Lands have been acquired, off-road vehicle events canceled, and veterinarians enlisted in attempts to protect the tortoise and its habitat.

ENDANGERED:
California
United States

PHOTOGRAPHED:
San Francisco
June 18, 1990

Desert Tortoise

Gopherus agassizii

ENDANGERED:
California
United States

PHOTOGRAPHED:
Kern County
July 21, 1988

Western Yellow-Billed Cuckoo

Coccyzus americanus occidentalis

This shy bird is more likely to be heard than seen. Identifiable by its song, a series of "kuks" followed by a series of "cows," it is a great lover of hairy caterpillars. As many as seventy thousand breeding pairs of the cuckoo once occupied riparian forests throughout the state. There are now fewer than fifty known nesting pairs. Only a restoration of riverside habitats will allow the yellow-billed cuckoo to survive.

San Francisco Garter Snake

Thamnophis sirtalis tetrataenia

The most radiant of the garter snakes, this species once ranged from northern San Mateo County to Ano Nuevo Point. Filled wetlands, diverted streams, roads, defoliated streambanks, and farmland have displaced most of its habitat. Cursed by its beauty, the shy reptile is also molested by outlaw snake collectors. It remains in only twenty known sites, in San Mateo County and the extreme north of Santa Cruz County. Luckily the San Francisco garter snake is protected in five state parks, where it is the object of federal and state recovery programs.

ENDANGERED:
California
United States

PHOTOGRAPHED: Fresno
July 27, 1987

60

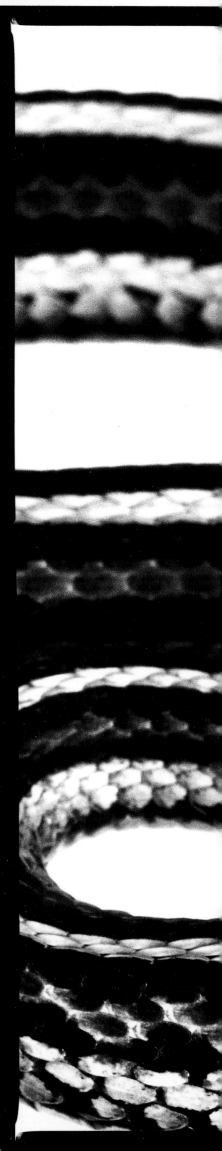

Pedate Checker-Mallow

Sidalcea pedata

ENDANGERED:
California
United States

PHOTOGRAPHED:
Bear Valley
May 23, 1988

This herb grows only in the unique "pavement" soils of wet alkaline meadows in the Big Bear Lake Basin in San Bernardino County. The meadows are extremely delicate and easily destroyed. The pedate checker-mallow once ranged throughout the Big Bear Lake Basin, but dam construction, drainage of wetlands, and water diversion have reduced its habitat to only three small sites totaling fourteen-and-a-half acres. All are privately owned. Residential development of these areas poses the most immediate threat to the plant's survival.

Pogogyne abramsii

San Diego Mesa Mint

Endemic to the mesas of extreme-southern California, the San Diego mesa mint was once common and widespread there. The plant is dependent on special microhabitats called vernal pools, which fill with rainwater in the winter and gradually dry through spring and summer. Most of these have been drained or converted to urban or agricultural lands, pushing the mesa mint close to extinction. Road construction tightens like a noose around its remaining habitat, severely threatening its chances for survival. The tiny, aromatic plant with reddish-purple flowers is also vulnerable to the tires of off-road vehicles, which tear plant cover from the soil in the three mesas where the plant remains.

ENDANGERED:
California
United States

PHOTOGRAPHED:
San Diego
April 24, 1988

Cordylanthus maritimus ssp. maritimus

Salt Marsh Bird's-Beak

ENDANGERED:
California
United States

PHOTOGRAPHED:
San Diego
April 22, 1988

This tidal wetland-dweller is a halophyte; it thrives in alkaline soils rich in sodium and calcium salts, which are inhospitable to most plants. Once growing in tidal wetlands all along the coast of Southern California and northern Baja California, the bird's-beak has been hard hit by the development of wetlands and the degradation of water quality by agricultural, residential, and industrial runoff. Much of the plant's remaining habitat lies on private lands, making protection difficult.

Slender-Horned Spineflower

Centrostegia leptoceras

The slender-horned spineflower, a member of the buckwheat family, grows in soils deposited where streams emerge from mountain ravines onto a flood plain. The community of plants that live on these alluvial fans are dependent on periodic floods to keep larger, woody growth from taking over. The slender-horned spineflower originally ranged throughout the Santa Ana River's flood plain terraces, but it is now limited to only five sites. This annual has lost most of its habitat to urban development and sand and gravel mining. Surviving plants, most of which are on private land and are unprotected, are threatened by flood control activities, competition from nonnative plants, off-road vehicles, and illegal trash dumping.

ENDANGERED:
California
United States

PHOTOGRAPHED:
San Bernardino
County
May 21, 1988

Giant Kangaroo Rat

ENDANGERED: California
United States

PHOTOGRAPHED: Bakersfield
May 19, 1988

Dipodomys ingens

The giant kangaroo rat relies on acute hearing and an elaborate network of burrows to elude coyotes, owls, and foxes on its nocturnal searches for seeds. It has another technique for eluding predators once they're close on its tail: It jumps and then, hurling the weight of its tail, spins in the air. When it hits the ground it's facing, and then running in, an unpredictable direction. The species once ranged the western San Joaquin Valley from Merced County south, on the Carrizo Plain, and in the Cuyama Valley. Agricultural development has run the rodent off of more than 95 percent of its original range, and recent studies show it in rapid decline throughout remaining portions of its habitat. Habitat protection holds the only hope for the giant kangaroo rat.

66

Erysimum capitatum var. angustatum

Contra Costa Wallflower

The Antioch Dunes, a sandy area near the juncture of the Sacramento and San Joaquin rivers, contain an astonishing number of plants, insects, and lizards unique to California. The Contra Costa wallflower is one of three endangered species endemic to the dunes. Sand mining, off-road vehicles, and industrial development have degraded or destroyed most of the original dunes.

Only 67 acres remain, and only 27 acres are pristine. In attempts to protect this unique habitat and the endangered species within it, a refuge has been set up by the U.S. Fish and Wildlife Service, and the Pacific Gas and Electric Company, which owns adjacent property, has agreed to protect the dunes occurring there.

ENDANGERED:
California
United States

PHOTOGRAPHED:
Antioch
March 15, 1990

THREATENED: California
United States

PHOTOGRAPHED:
Ring Mountain, Marin County
June 19, 1987

Unique to Ring Mountain, this late-
blooming lily is found on a serpentine
grassland on the mountain's north slope.
The area is owned and managed by The
Nature Conservancy, which has barred off-
road vehicles from the site and had nur-
tured the lily population from a thousand
plants in 1982 to ten thousand in 1987.
The Tiburon mariposa lily is the only
California plant ever downlisted from an
endangered species to a threatened one.

Tiburon Mariposa Lily

Calochortus tiburonensis

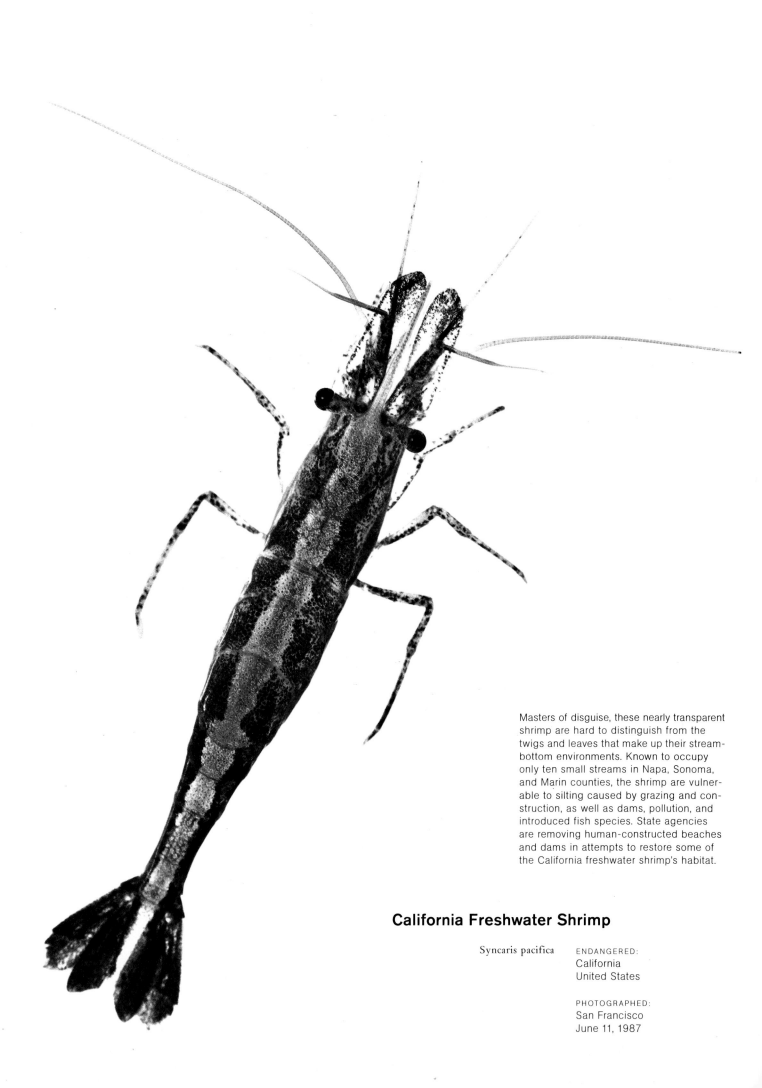

Masters of disguise, these nearly transparent
shrimp are hard to distinguish from the
twigs and leaves that make up their stream-
bottom environments. Known to occupy
only ten small streams in Napa, Sonoma,
and Marin counties, the shrimp are vulnerable to silting caused by grazing and construction, as well as dams, pollution, and
introduced fish species. State agencies
are removing human-constructed beaches
and dams in attempts to restore some of
the California freshwater shrimp's habitat.

California Freshwater Shrimp

Syncaris pacifica   ENDANGERED:
California
United States

PHOTOGRAPHED:
San Francisco
June 11, 1987

Baker's Meadowfoam   *Limnanthes bakeri*

When its seeds are crushed Baker's meadowfoam produces a valuable oil similar to sperm whale oil. It is found in fewer than a dozen sites in the saturated clay soils of meadowlands in Mendocino County, all of them on private lands.

Grazing, residential development, and altered drainage patterns threaten the remaining plants. The Nature Conservancy lobbies landowners to protect meadowfoam where they find it on their property.

RARE: California
CANDIDATE: United States

PHOTOGRAPHED:
Mendocino County
May 2, 1987

Blunt-Nosed Leopard Lizard

Gambelia sila

The fierce blunt-nosed leopard lizard changes color to help regulate its body temperature. Spots and bars on the lizard's back are dark in the morning and lighten as the day warms. Males turn a light pinkish color when courting; females show rust-orange spots along their sides after they have mated. *Gambelia sila* once ranged throughout much of the San Joaquin Valley, but 95 percent of this area has been developed, mostly for farming. Federal, state, and local agencies are setting aside lands as part of a recovery plan for the lizard.

ENDANGERED: California
United States

PHOTOGRAPHED:
Bakersfield
May 20, 1988

Blunt-Nosed Leopard Lizard, *Gambelia sila*

Great Gray Owl

Strix nebulosa

The longest North American owl, the great gray once swooped silently throughout the Sierra Nevada and north coast, launching itself from treetops with a beat of huge wings. But logging has removed most of its preferred old-growth forest habitats, and grazing sheep and cattle have destroyed many of the mountain meadows the owl needs for its diet of voles and pocket gophers. In 1988 only ten breeding pairs of great gray owls were known, all of them in or near Yosemite National Park. The total statewide population may now be as low as sixty individuals.

ENDANGERED: California
United States

PHOTOGRAPHED: San Francisco
May 1, 1987

Ovis canadensis nelsoni

Desert Bighorn Sheep

NOT CURRENTLY LISTED
PHOTOGRAPHED: Los Angeles
June 24, 1988

Bighorn sheep, historically a favorite target of game hunters, are skittish and extremely wary of human beings, and therefore difficult to approach. There are three subspecies of bighorns in the mountains of Southern California. The one pictured here is luckier than its cousins, the California and the peninsular bighorn sheep. Both of them are endangered, victims of livestock-spread diseases and destruction of their watering holes by introduced burros. *Nelsoni* has been successfully isolated from feral burros and livestock, and has been aided with artificial water supplies. Its populations have stabilized and some regulated hunting of *nelsoni* is even permitted.

California's tiger salamanders spend most
of the year waiting underground, usually in
the burrows of other animals, leaving their
retreats for only a few days or weeks at
a time and heading, in mass nighttime
migrations, for breeding ponds. Much of
the salamander's historical habitat in the
lower foothills of the Sierra Nevada has
been lost to urban and agricultural
development.

California Tiger Salamander

Ambystoma californieuse

SPECIES OF SPECIAL CONCERN: California
CANDIDATE: United States

PHOTOGRAPHED: San Francisco
September 16, 1987

80

COLOR PORTRAITS

< COACHELLA VALLEY FRINGE-TOED LIZARD
Uma inornata

LIGHT-FOOTED CLAPPER RAIL
Rallus longirostris levipes

scale 1.0x

scale .80x

LITTLE KERN GOLDEN TROUT
Oncorhynchus aquabonita whitei

scale .80x

Western Lily

Lilium occidentale

scale .30x

NORTH AMERICAN RIVER OTTER
Lutra canadensis

scale .33x

BAREFOOT BANDED GECKO
Coleonyx switaki

scale 1.8x

San Joaquin Antelope Squirrel
Ammospermophilus nelsoni

scale 1.2x

GEYSERS' PANICUM

Dichanthelium lanuginosum var. *thermale*

scale 2.7x

THE SAN FRANCISCO FORKTAIL DAMSELFLY
Ischnura gemina

Valley Oak
Quercus lobata

scale .005x

AMERICAN PEREGRINE FALCON
Falco peregrinus anatum

scale .50x

BLACK TOAD

Bufo exsul

scale 4.7x

Salt Marsh Harvest Mouse
Reithrodontomys raviventris

scale 3.0x

CALIFORNIA BROWN PELICAN
Pelecanus occidentalis californicus

Santa Ana River Woollystar
Eriastrum densifolium ssp. *sanctorum*

scale .33x

SHASTA CRAYFISH
Pacifastacus fortis

scale 2.0x

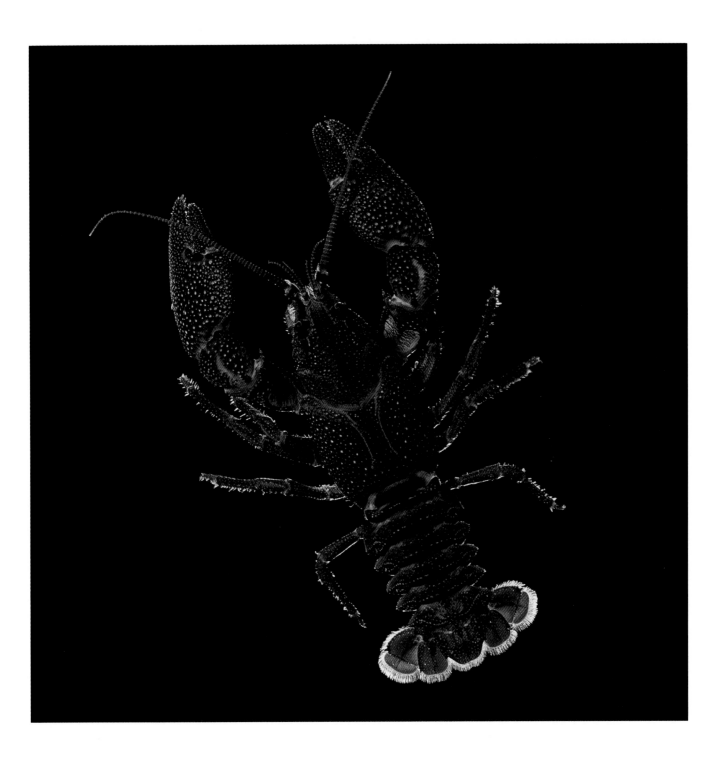

ROUGH SCULPIN
Cottus asperrimus

scale 3.0x

BAKERSFIELD CACTUS
Opuntia basilaris var. *treleasei*

scale 1.5x

ANTIOCH DUNES EVENING-PRIMROSE
Oenothera deltoides var. *howellii*

scale .60x

8 50 03   8 50 10   8 50 17

8 50 24   8 50 31   8 50 38

8 50 45   8 50 52   8 50 59

May 15, 1990 8:50PM 03 to 59 seconds

Desert Tortoise
Gopherus agassizii

scale .80x

WESTERN YELLOW-BILLED CUCKOO
Coccyzus americanus occidentalis

scale 1.2x

San Francisco Garter Snake
Thamnophis sirtalis tetrataenia

scale (top left) .50x

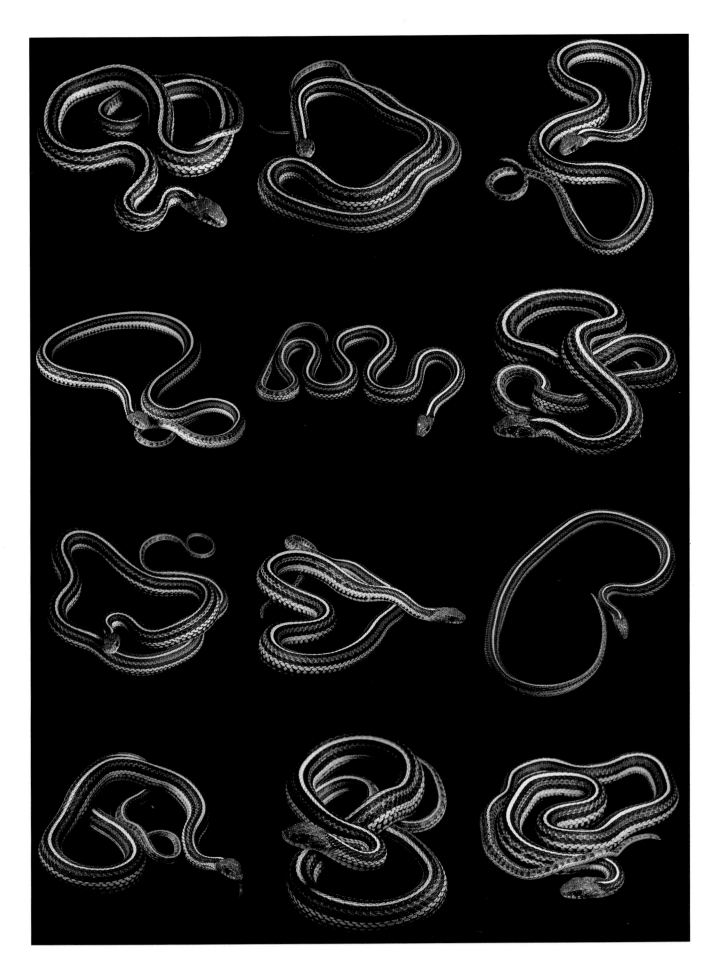

+ SAN DIEGO MESA MINT
    Pogogyne abramsii

+ SLENDER-HORNED SPINEFLOWER
    Centrostegia leptoceras

+ SALT MARSH BIRD'S-BEAK
    Cordylanthus maritimus ssp. *maritimus*

+ PEDATE CHECKER-MALLOW
    Sidalcea pedata

scale 5.0x

scale 7.8x

scale 2.3x

scale 2.6x

GIANT KANGAROO RAT
Dipodomys ingens

scale 1.3x

CONTRA COSTA WALLFLOWER
Erysimum capitatum var. *angustatum*

scale .20x

Tiburon Mariposa Lily
Calochortus tiburonensis

scale 3.0x

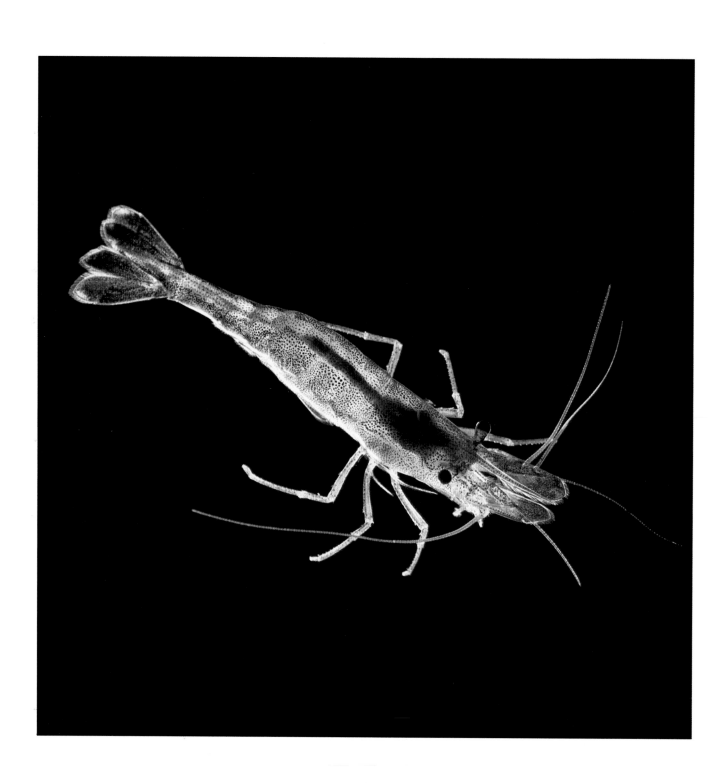

<< CALIFORNIA FRESHWATER SHRIMP
Syncaris pacifica

< BAKER'S MEADOWFOAM
Limnanthes bakeri

BLUNT-NOSED LEOPARD LIZARD
Gambelia sila

scale 3.5x

scale 7.0x

scale 1.0x

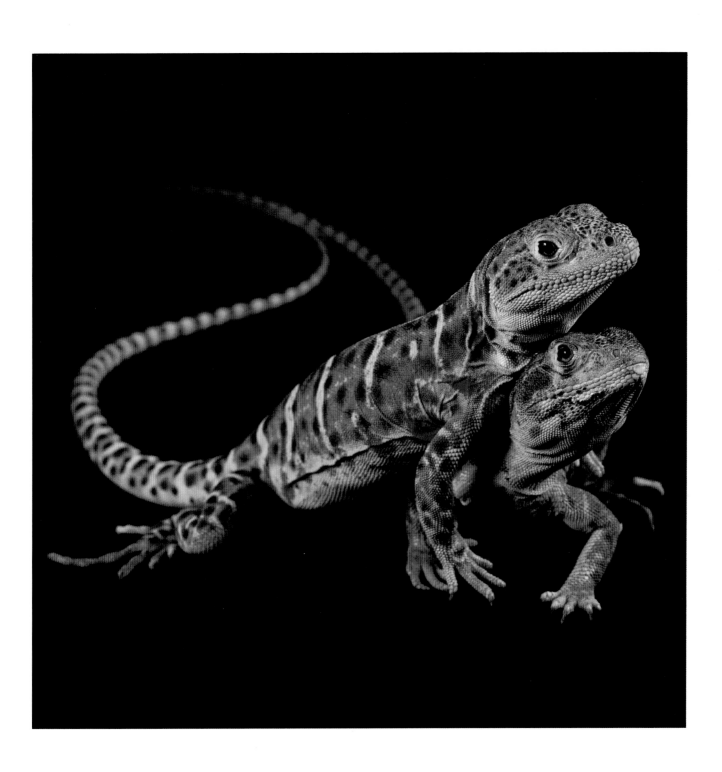

GREAT GRAY OWL
Strix nebulosa

scale 8.0x

DESERT BIGHORN SHEEP
Ovis canadensis nelsoni

scale .40x male

scale .30x female

Glossary

The somewhat complex concept of species endangerment draws its force from the blunt and simple reality of extinction. Similarly, the designations used by the federal and state wildlife agencies describe degrees of closeness to the ultimate designation, EXTINCT SPECIES —which needs little explanation. Other listing designations are cited in the previous pages, and they are generally defined as follows:

ENDANGERED: A species in serious danger of becoming extinct throughout all, or a significant portion of, its range.

THREATENED: A species that, although not presently threatened with extinction, is likely to become an endangered species in the foreseeable future unless conservation steps are taken.

RARE: A plant species that, although not presently threatened with extinction, survives in such small numbers that it may become endangered if its environment worsens.

CANDIDATE: A species that has been formally proposed and is under consideration for possible listing as an endangered or threatened species.

SPECIES OF SPECIAL CONCERN: A species that warrants special conservation treatment in the view of the California Department of Fish and Game. This is an administrative designation (as opposed to a formal, legal designation under the Endangered Species Act) intended to prevent species from becoming THREATENED or ENDANGERED by addressing their problems before their long-term viability is jeopardized.

COMMUNITY OF SPECIAL CONCERN: A plant community that warrants special conservation treatment in the view of the California Department of Fish and Game. Also an administrative listing, this is similar to the SPECIES OF SPECIAL CONCERN designation except that it applies to entire plant communities. One hundred and fifty two of the total 375 natural plant communities in California are COMMUNITIES OF SPECIAL CONCERN.

In 1973 the U.S. Congress passed the Endangered Species Act, directing the Secretaries of the Interior and Commerce to protect any plant or animal found, on the basis of scientific evidence alone, to be threatened with extinction. The signing of this legislation marked an essential change in our relationship with, and official responsibility to, the species with which we share this planet.

Congress couldn't have predicted the ramifications of the legislation. When it was passed the act was expected to apply to only a few hundred species. Today there are more than a thousand species on the federal threatened and endangered lists and more than three thousand others are under serious consideration for listing in the United States alone. Once a species has been designated endangered or threatened the act prohibits (with only a few narrow exceptions) anyone from killing it, capturing it, or otherwise harming it. The act also mandates that a plan be developed and realized to aid the species' recovery.

California established its own Endangered Species Act in 1970. Although it parallels the federal act in many ways, it focuses on preserving California's endemic endangered species as well as preserving species endangered in California but doing well elsewhere. For this reason the federal and state lists share an area of overlap but are not identical. Similarly the listing designations used by the state and federal government mean basically the same things, but have different consequences reflecting their different jurisdictional and administrative responsibilities.

Though the endangered species list reflects the state of the natural world, it is an imperfect mirror: its surface is marred by politics, economics, and the material limits of the agencies overseeing it. Since the act was passed, an unknown number of species have become extinct without even being considered for inclusion on the list. More than three hundred CANDIDATE species throughout the United States have become extinct while waiting for their listing applications to be processed.

Technical Notes

by David Liittschwager

All the photographs in this book were taken with Hasselblad cameras. The lenses we used the most were the 135mm S-Plannar and the 150mm Sonnar. For the largest subject, the valley oak, we used the 50mm Distagon. We lit the oak with electronic flash: eight flash heads powered by three 2,400-watt-second power packs times six exposures. The black background was the dark of night. For the smallest subject, the Slender-Horned Spineflower, we used a 55mm Micro-Nikkor, reversed on an automatic bellows at full extension. Again we used electronic flash: one 400-watt-second flash head with a fiber-optic attachment to provide the precision needed when working so small. Most of the other plants were lit by the sun. The animals were lit with electronic flash.

Most of the color photographs in this book were taken on Kodak Ektachrome 100. For the black and white photographs we used Kodak Panatomic-X processed in D-76 and Agfa-pan 100 processed in Rodinal. We used a Minolta Flash Meter III to determine the exposure except when to do so would disturb the subject. In such cases we used Polaroid Type 669 or 665. The black and white prints were made on Agfa Insignia paper with Simmons Omega D2 enlarger, using a condenser or cold-light head.

Photographing endangered plants and animals presents some special problems. When working with plants that grow in clusters we avoided damaging them by constructing a raised platform on which to work and by inserting, from above, a small background to isolate the subject.

Each animal required a different setup. The damselflies were placed in a small box that was attached to the lens. We photographed the golden trout in an aquarium designed to keep the fish within the range of focus while they swam about. Rough sculpins are bottom-dwelling fishes, so their aquarium had a seamless transition from floor to back wall. It was necessary to stay within surroundings familiar to the bighorn sheep, as they are very high strung. We photographed them in the barn where they spend their nights. It was a challenge to keep the raptors calm. A dimly lit, empty room with a single perch worked best.

Primrose time, mouse time, and cuckoo time are not human time. An evening-primrose blossom lasts a single night. A salt marsh mouse lives for nine months. A yellow-billed cuckoo must feed its young once every hour. Observing and adapting to the time schemes of these lives was one of the project's great joys.

San Francisco Forktail Damselfly
May 28, 1988

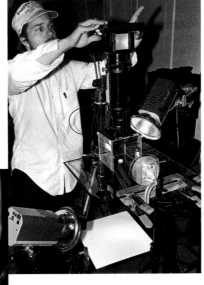

Salt Marsh Harvest Mouse
October 23, 1990

ACKNOWLEDGEMENTS

142

We would like to express our deepest gratitude to the many people who helped us during the last five years and made this book possible.

Our thanks to the entire staff of the California Academy of Sciences for their continuing support,
The California Nature Conservancy, especially Kelly Cash, for believing in this project at its inception,
Alison Silverstein and Pacific Gas and Electric Company for supporting the continuation of the project.

To WHITNEY LOWE, the designer, for his vision and perseverance.

To GORDY SLACK for his editorial expertise, patience, and good humor.

To the CALIFORNIA ACADEMY OF SCIENCES research scientists
for checking the text: Frank Almeda, Steve Bailey, Dusty Chivers,
Bill Eschmeyer, Terry Gosliner, Dave Kavanaugh,
Alan Leviton, John McCosker, Jens Vindum.

To Lesley Bruynesteyn and Jack Jensen
at CHRONICLE BOOKS for wanting to make this book.

To WENDELL and TANYA BERRY for their contribution during lamb birthing time on the farm.

To BARRY LOPEZ for his encouragement and insight.

To Richard Avedon FOR HIS CONVICTION,
Lydia Modi Vitale FOR HER PASSIONATE COMMITMENT TO EXCELLENCE,
AND Paul Hoffman FOR HIS PATIENT EAR.

To the following people who contributed their energy, talent, and friendship:

Ruedi Hofmann   Robert Seidler
Demetrios Scourtis   Nicholas Taylor
Rodney Marzullo   Blake Summers
Mary Richardson and Theodore   Tamara Freedman
The Richardson families   Peter Cunningham
Richard Bodner and family   Mary Ellen Mark
Terry and Jody Grundy   Martin Bell
Ann Giordano   Suzanne Fritch
Marc Charnow   William Emery
Jan Lundberg   Carol Anderson
Caroline Kopp   Kirk Frederick
Tom Marioni and the MOCA group   Roy Eisenhardt

In memory of those who gave us love and support during their short time on Earth:
Mick Ward, Jay Tverdak, Maureen Minton, Michael Finden, Frank Loverde, Bill Oliver, Ivory Wesley, & Richard Winslow.

We want to thank the following organizations and individuals for assisting in the photography and production: CALIFORNIA NATURAL DIVERSITY DATA BASE, CALIFORNIA LIVING MUSEUM, CALIFORNIA DEPARTMENT OF FISH AND GAME, FRESNO ZOO, HAMMER FARMS, LOS ANGELES ZOO, MUSEUM OF VERTEBRATE ZOOLOGY AT THE UNIVERSITY OF CALIFORNIA/BERKELEY, SAN DIEGO SEA WORLD, SAN FRANCISCO ZOO, SANTA CRUZ PREDATORY BIRD RESEARCH GROUP, TIJUANA NATIONAL WILDLIFE ESTUARY, U.S. FISH AND WILDLIFE SERVICE, AND ERNST WILDI OF VICTOR HASSELBLAD INCORPORATED.

JIM MCKINNEY	BECKWITH THOMPSON	PHIL PISTER	JEFF LEVIN
JOHN AIKIN	THOM KATO	DAN CHRISTENSEN	DIANE MITCHELL
THEO LIGHT	CAROL KATO	JIM DEFORGE	LLOYD KIFF
TOM HESSELDENZ	GARY PARKER	LYDIA FRAZIER	JOHN HAFERNIK
KENT REEVES	KEVIN HUNTING	THE BENHAMS	SEAN MCKEOWN
LISA B. WAYNE	JOYCE HUNTING	GARY PRIEST	BILL ASSERSON
SALLY DEBECKER	DAWN SMITH	CHRIS PETERSON	JOHN BRODE
STEWART HINDLEY	MAILE NEEL	PAUL JORGENSON	JOHN GUSTAFSON
CHARLOTTE FIORITO	SYLVIA RUST	KAREN SAUSMAN	LAIRD MARSHALL
JAMIE TANAKA	FRANK RUST	TERRY KRAAL	STAN STEVENS
STEPHEN CLAWSON	JOHN HAMMER	BETTY GRISELL	BOB STAFFORD
TODD ECKERT	STEVE LAYMON	MARK WEITZLE	PETER STEEL
CHRIS KREUGER	PAULA KLIER	TOM OBERBAUER	RON TILLER
AMY PERTSCHUK	BEN DIAL	GERI HULSE-STEVENS	LYNN LOZIER
BRIAN COLLENTINE	BRIAN WALTON	DAVE IMPER	LARRY SERPA

We are especially grateful to our parents for their love and sustenance: *JEAN MIDDLETON, FRAN WILLIAMS, TERRY LIITTSCHWAGER.* And to *SUZIE RASHKIS* for her ideas and companionship.

Most importantly, we are indebted to those plants and animals who were the inspiration for this project.

Index